Queen and Carcass

Queen and Carcass

Anna van Valkenburg

an imprint of Anvil Press

"a feed dog book" for Anvil Press

Anvil Press Publishers Inc.
P.O. Box 3008, Station Terminal
Vancouver, BC V6B 3X5
www.anvilpress.com

Imprint editor: Stuart Ross
Cover design: Rayola.com
Interior design & typesetting: Stuart Ross
Author photo: Adam Grabowski
feed dog logo: Catrina Longmuir

Library and Archives Canada Cataloguing in Publication

Title: Queen & carcass / Anna van Valkenburg.
Other titles: Queen and carcass
Names: Van Valkenburg, Anna, author.
Description: Poems.
Identifiers: Canadiana 20200314653 | ISBN 9781772141696 (softcover)
Classification: LCC PS8643.A599 Q44 2020 | DDC C811/.6—dc23

Printed and bound in Canada

Represented in Canada by Publishers Group Canada
Distributed in Canada by Raincoast Books; in the U.S. by Small Press Distribution (SPD)

The publisher gratefully acknowledges the financial assistance of the Canada Council for the Arts, the Canada Book Fund, and the Province of British Columbia through the B.C. Arts Council and the Book Publishing Tax Credit.

CONTENTS

I

Abracadabra!

There will be no greater pain.

This will make you human.

—Jezibaba, Act I, *Rusalka*

MELODIES

In the thin whistle of a train
that passed through the station
without stopping

I hear Aunt Krystyna
defeathering a white hen
in her courtyard, in the shadow
of a heap of clouds.

Dry concrete,
a praying box of marguerites,
and the shiny blade cooling off
on a stump of brick.

The stick feet work as a metronome
going up and down,
up, down,
as she plucks the body
against her body. She's in tune

with the rhythm of the wind
knocking on the tin shed,
the buzz of the power lines
that stretch around her yard,
the lazy mewls of cats
plugging holes
too costly to fix.

She plucks without losing tempo,
without getting carried
in the swell of a moment's
pleasure that rises and loafs
before hungry eyes.

Even the clouds drop from the sky
like a pair of trousers, baring
what's underneath.

To this, Aunt Krystyna
looks up, unconcerned
at the lowering tray of mist,
and the hen doesn't
squirm or cackle, just flects
to her loosened fist.

She is at once queen
and carcass.

The thought of this leaves me
swelling like a balloon.
I lift up in song.

MY FIRST HOME ASKS TO BE REMEMBERED

The street knocks on my door.

It's the middle of the night, and it's asking
for milk. For a quarter of my life I haven't craved
fire or sparkle. I haven't sucked on its flame
and now it's weightless.
My memory, too, is ill
and ruffled—it looks out through the door
but doesn't sing. Oh, maybe if the street
would rock from side to side. Maybe
if the street would start to bend
at the knees, sway its giant hips,
whistle through its wet lips. It could jolt
the birds awake in the trees. Stealthily,

I wait for a gesture.
I drink what I can.

BINOCULARS

The pink man who kept a weasel
on a leash sat outside
his stucco house, losing pigment
in the sun and gathering gossip. We called him
lorneta—binoculars.

My aunt Basia and I
took turns giving him news
that crawled like wild weeds
into our ears,
out of purses and cellars,
from stoves and bathtubs,
from the neglected corners
of our neighbours' mouths.

That hot and acrid summer, we longed
to go to Ślesin Beach
to put our toes in the scraggly water.
The air hung drier each day, the grass crept to the shade.
Basia and I carried leather flip-flops
and saggy swimsuits in our shoulder bags.
We had skinny arms and legs.

But how quickly we grew! On the last day of summer,
the sky darkened. We ran
from the bus station toward the house. It rained.
Lorneta flashed us a glance, and we'd have sworn
he would crash like thunder down the street.

We hid in the bathroom all evening
that day, sleeking
our frizzed hair with butterfly clips.

I wanted to cool off in the shower,
and found a cockroach on my towel.
Aunt Basia washed it down the sink with scalding water
and stunned, I wondered, will it come back
up? It won't, it won't, she said,
only people do that.

THE IMAGINARY TOWN OF GRIMM

after Venus Khoury-Ghata

I.   While living in Grimm
I learned that sailors get cold sores
when the wind blows from the east,

and duck rash when the summer
knots itself around their paddling legs,

but still they come face-to-face
with the heat wave's rising sun.

II.   I learned that poppies sway, rock-bound,
when the wind opens up its mouth
like a whale in the orchestral ocean.

But it would take a proper whiplash
to pull a poppy away from the field.

III.   I see the people scurry about,
their days longer, their dusty fears
folded into bread. They work

on all fours in salt mines, in circuses
—black teeth wedged into red meat.

IV.   After they killed the milk goat
to stockpile for rainy days
they tore open dusk.

For a while, the field
got richer. When it
overgrew the laundry lines,
it knit sweaters with corn stalks.

One day, it brushed
against the sun, caught fire.

It couldn't blow itself out.
It cooked a feast on its own flame.

V.   Before the dry spell, the town was red, over-
flowing with rhubarb and grass
that cut your feet if you ran through it;
with smoke that curled like the pink tails
of mud-pigs; with pencil-sharp bees;
spiders climbing through open windows;
rain that left chills.

VI.   A town is a tin of children
in an ocean.

VII.   They've built a new milk goat
out of wire, stuffed it with hay.
She breaks at the sight of a hill
though she has never slipped from a mountain;
at the sight of a puddle, though she has
never risked drowning.

VIII.   An ocean is an island. That's a choice.

IX.   The smothered children
spring out in crescendo;

then airily
collapse into the dust.

X.   The rock cracks like bread crust
between two hands.
They arrive hungry;

pull at the root with steel arms
until it comes loose
and disorients them.

CITADEL

Then, whenever I ran down to the cellar
to gather jars of compote, damp clothes
from the washer, red beets
in netted sacks, it stood like a beast
in black rain; I froze breath-
less in the door frame, doe eye to red eye.
I had to ask the boiler to let me live.

Now I visit only too aware:
we don't need supplies, no one is afraid
and there is no tragedy
in the world that warrants
jarring fruit for the winter.

There are no barbarians on the lawn
with turnips in their pockets,
only men in suits with sunshine
up their sleeves. I am the only one
who needs this cellar.

I beg the boiler to let me for God's sake
keep asking if I am alive.
His bright eye shines
toward a long bright future.

No, that's not what I'm asking—

LETTER FROM A REAL TOWN: I

I ask the town
since I had left
why it had gone

to the alien
tongues that ballooned
in speech but pruned
in the mouth
at the sight of tubs of lard
and pickled vegetables.

It says that even parents
can't wait forever
for children to come

home. It leaves me
spitting up
on a dry mound
of gravel;

not quite
stiff as a grave,
but almost.

CULTURE

It growls amid bushes
and stone. It growls
in the trees.

Varmint is like this as well.

Wet kindling.

A library
in a language
no one can read.

ECOLOGY IN DREAM FORM

When you are teaching me to navigate our new-found country, I dream someone else is writing us into a forest glade. Patches of light and dew. The rustling chirr of wood-pewees, the bustle of critters. Open air. You start at the white bed sheet, a flag of skin between us, and I feel the immense sky in the waking smell of summer. Hollyhock and violets, hipbones and breasts. Both of us small, wild things.

LETTER TO A REAL TOWN: II

Forest land of blue-
berries and wolves,
meadow mice, moss,
sparkling lakes,

balance,
democracy,
health:

some part of you is always off
searching for love
in my head.

I am George,
you, Lennie.
What of human nature:
I won't know about regret
until you're gone.

HARD TRUTH

Even when we fought

off the enemy, and later

cauterized its wounds

with gunpowder,

our love shut its eyes

and refused

to keep living. It was

wiser than either of us

could ever be.

It said,

"I am a martyr.

Martyrs die."

LETTERS FROM A NATIVE TONGUE

I lie with closed eyes under the roof of your mouth.
Some light blows in from the east.
Only looks like a sky, but it's not endless, you say.

I've been trying to give in to sleep ever since
you found an alternate route
for your words.

From the Vistula
to the Nile

the men in your head are hard at work
building larger, sturdier ships.

Do I ask to be jolted?

I flip toward your throat. Even there
darkness is scarce, solitude a thin whistle.

I want to drain out every bell, every hammer-
hit, every spark. But each time

I come close to losing consciousness,
the stars of the alphabet drive into me
on the train tracks of your vocal cords.

RUSALKA AS ARTIST

A light strand of hair sketches
the outline of your walnut
face. You fracture the wind
that sifts through the net
like water. I shift in my place.

There they speak of butterflies
the size of birds, and of you
leaving scarlet spots on each
of their wings. What of words:
they say you collected them
only to snap their brittle
branches mid-air.

On a stump by the lake
a man paints under the same sun
that burned my thighs and contoured
your features, blurred the right ridges
and burnished them.
Your torso and legs twisted
into the most siren positions
in that light. Only one arm
stayed out of it: you needed it to create.

There, in the running water, a collapsed tree
under the same sun.
I wondered if you had broken it
as a gift to the creator.

My first time seeing you move
was on canvas;
my body fluttered, a blade of grass
between two thumbs and moist lips.
Since then, I've wanted to climb
into the poster with the boy
who makes a little globe with his fingers.
He is holding the world. I mimic him.
I want you to climb in and sleep there.
So what if it leaves you thin as sketch paper
and emulsified in the wrong colour—
so long as I hold you, I am still
blushing.

A PORTRAIT OF SERVING GIRLS
AS NIGHTINGALES

The serving girls argue
over who will collect the eggs
from the chicken coop

and from his bed
the master hears them.
The white moon has swung

over the roof and
split open dusk.
It is a dream I am having

more and more and more:

a rooster spits devotions into the sky's
sleeping throat
then loses his head;

the cows have shed their shadows
under the juniper and slither
into the pastures;

what was dark turns darker
in the sun.
It is a dream I am having

but it is happening now: know,
inside these girls, there are

one thousand others
carrying the peeps

and squawks of every
bird that dared
snatch a currant

from a thorny bush. They say
the teeth can be a gate-
way to the truth.

Know, inside those girls
there are one
thousand others.

Now here,
through the door—

a crack
in the light. And sleep
in their mouths.

In the corner
of an unnamed room,
they wait

for a piece of fruit.

DAWN AT THE EDGE OF THE WOODS

Two trees, peeking out
from two thousand years ago
are bored with each other.

They spot me
—in my kitchen
lined with potted lavender,

verbena, dill—
from behind the peacock-
green fence. I'm stirring up matcha

with cane sugar
and coconut milk.
They nudge each other

in the ribs, knock on the glass
with crooked knuckles,
call me to come in, come in!

In the forest: birdsong;
blueberries and chanterelles
line the woodland's edge;

violets, bluebells and
redbud; one big bad wolf;
two drowned nymphs.

How generous! To witness living history
with my own big eyes—
what splendour!

But don't they know the bit
about keeping a distance
from unfamiliar girls?

Girls have an appetite
for trees; their fangs
cut through bark.

Just when I'm about to
leap out the window, open
my green mouth in response,

Eve walks in on me, tells
me to keep my clothes on,
definitely my panties—

these trees are all the same
and we've been here before.

KNOWLEDGE

A thought is born
in the vast ether.
A century later
a city is in ruins
and that was the city
where a golden cherub
stood at attention
on the edge of a burning
university
screaming at the men: More,
more fire!
Learn more!
Learn faster!

LESSONS

The girl comes in from the cold, tells me:
My feet are bigger than yours.

I don't bat an eyelash, and she repeats:
Bigger than yours, my feet
are bigger than yours.
What will you do now?

I look down at my regular-sized feet.
I guess I'll live with them, I say
but she doesn't concede.

How will you live with them?
They must be far too small,
they are at least smaller than mine.

And that is when I gain perspective—
she is right. The toes are thin
in comparison, the bottoms frail and pale.

The ankles are slim,
the length doesn't even compare.

My feet are small—smaller than hers at least—
and I don't know how I will live
with myself.

LITTLE RED IN LOVE

Before the fire ate up our houses
like silver bags of crispy chips,
one plank of wood after another—

our houses tall blondes
with lipstick, match-
stick legs—

we ran the ravines
and banks of the creek

collecting: old lighters,
shards of green glass,
the bones of dead birds,
leaves shaped like apples
and worms.

The scent of tobacco
made nests in our hair.

We kissed sloppily,
gave each other flowers.

You left poppies on my chest:
black teeth surrounded
by red petals;

I left you cornflowers.

*

I'm the bone in the soup,
the dog's dark feet
after rain; what remains
when the second letter of the alphabet
bites the first while waiting its turn,
and the mother throws a scowl
like *How could you ever think*
you could talk to a wolf
and get away with it?

LOOKING DOWN ZAKOLE STREET

A streak of people crowds the sidewalk from the pharmacy to the Billiard & Disco, and I stand still, remembering a single shadow I had almost missed; it gnawed itself free from the wall and slid through the grass, past the soviet-style low blocks, the iron swings, the bottles in the street, and straight into a rabbit hole. Was it a smudge of thick black smoke or the tattered echo of a dog's red bark? Was it a baby sun playing tricks on me? For the longest time, my mind is dusty as an alleyway. When I hear the wall screaming, it may be a riot I remember, and the next time I do, I paint a mural over it: a crowded city street— men, children, dogs, and soldiers holding clouds of balloons in their teeth. And two women, unannounced, making their way through the meat of the crowd in the hardened sunlight. One chews a toothpick, one nothing. One of them looks like me— one doesn't.

LETTER TO A REAL TOWN: III

I became a woman
when revolution
was taking a nap
on the windowsill.
The men were dying from stasis.
The hands of the clock marched
drunkenly through the streets,
directionless.

Of this body
there will remain only
what has passed through it.
Even still,
I like to set one or two birds' eggs in my empty
bed, and say, in a voice
like a street lamp,
like a shadow: in me
you have something from which
there is no falling.

THE THORN AND THE WASHBASIN

If they could fly, there'd be no men on earth, prababcia says
to the knees in the cropland, the nettles encircling her wrists
like a garland. Her scarf is still nearly red. In the shadow
of the Ursus 360 it pinches off her head.

I've bled red like that between my fingers
plucking gooseberries like guitar strings,
plopping them into the same powder-blue washbasin
that ran dark like a mud river
where the plastic was scratched; that withstood the weight

of all the fallen offspring
of the cherry tree,
of the milky reflection
of the moon,
of candles, genuflections,
of the last rain,

until it cracked, became un-
recognizable to itself.

I imagine her as a kestrel without arms.
I'm a kestrel and she's a kestrel
but the sky isn't made
for kestrels but humans,

and suddenly
the earth flips, falling into
her eyes like rows upon rows
of harvest soil. We have
no hands to wipe it away.
I blow air in her eyes,
but this doesn't empty them.
I rub her eyes with leaves.

Ringed worms wrap around her
neck and her rib cage,
twice around each leg.

She shoots up into
the budding sky.

II

When you come back this way
the blooms will be red roses.
The white flowers were first
to wilt in the hot sun.

—Chorus, Act II, *Rusalka*

SNOW WHITE GIVES BIRTH TO AN APPLE

White meat in her hands,
in her belly sweetness.

One day the distance

between
myself and you
will disappear.

STEADY FLASHES

Even your mother blinks
her eyes open
when crying;

makes sure
you are watching

*

red, a fire

hydrant breaks

pissing small squirts

the limbless dog

slogs by

*

at the table, you thought

if you had a mouth
full of emeralds

you couldn't eat.

A FROZEN PLUM TELLS TIME

Yesterday you hid in the corner of a room
and you were happy.

Today you hid between the sheets, a soft babe.
You were happy as well.

Do you feel the chill of time? It's a frozen plum.
When it thaws it will be edible

again, you will have to deal with it then.
I think you are already thinking

about where you will hide tomorrow.
I know what I'm thinking: I'll be happy if you hide

where I can find you,
and if the plum will remain frozen a moment longer

this time. Slowly, slowly it will come round
to room temperature.

I will be perfectly happy wiping the table of its residue
once I have found you.

FERN & GARDENER

It was the first time you worked— .
the last time you didn't

see a fern sprouting at the right time.
In the depths of the woods,

you fed it bites of rain and blew white
clouds of breath when the sun shone.

You rearranged the trees
when mice and bullfinches came

hungry. Still, the spore slept in the shadows
between its before and its after.

Still tucked away
in a distant winter dream.

When you first worked
you accepted that

the fern wouldn't grow
into a fern before

it was ready.
Regardless of you

and your working hands,
but needing them.

HOLDUP

Gloves, you've been dispossessed
of your red hands
and in the square you've been

rounded up
with the other possessions
of jailed men;

a watch has lost
its tick,

a shoelace lies
unravelled

on a white unopened letter.
Not a single breath can be caught
leaving its lung.

As they watch
from behind their bars,
you form yours.

AFTER WAR

On the coldest of clear days in the vast landscape
smoke rises from the chimneys of the sugar factory

beneath the hard pale sun. Workers swarm in
from village houses, from city buses;

smoke spills into the clouds
like sweet condensed air from a tin can;

a pull from a giant cigarette, so badly
needed that morning, so badly exhaled.

I didn't know
the sky
was tarpaulin.

ANIMAL PARK

In a park named after a famous composer,
I toss the last wedge of dried bread.

The snorts and neighs have quieted.
It's all done, I think.

The donkeys gleam
in the sun like marble statues,

the hogs lounge across a canvas
of mud and mouldering potatoes.

It seems there is nothing to do
except gather my last thoughts to leave,

but as I fold the plastic bag
back into my pocket,

recalling my route to the iron gate
past the emus and peacocks

through the play park,
the grey sky unrolls

into a clashing symphony:
an ancient flood falling

into my open palms
once filled with plumes of sun.

And it strikes me:

in every note there are
those who remember

once walking these paths;
who didn't notice they were dead.

SLEEP

We should close our eyes now

to hear the rain scurrying through the trough
the chicks rearranging on the roost
the wind and well-water clambering
together in the bucket

under the moon's watchful eye

the hallway begins at the front door and ends
at the candle sconce
the wristwatch of the night

when the flame flickers out
our father
a blue sheep
will come
and we will sleep
until birth.

A CHILD DIED

They tossed his body into a potato bag
and took turns slinging it over their shoulders
until the exercise was over.

The body, identified upon death as male,
but never by name, was buried

in a place unknown. Somebody went to prison—

they thrust his body between bars
and took turns checking on it
till the sentence was over.

The body was identified definitively
by name, nationality, temperament.
Nobody would ever misplace it.

ON PERSPECTIVE

Lost. Lost in grey space.
Morning, they disperse
among the furniture
in this small, dusty apartment.
In the Odyssey, they travelled the same way:
battling the elements, the forces of the gods,
to reach Ithaca.

They gather the crumbs of bread
they have found, the fallen remains
of peeled potatoes and carrots,
and disappear under the couch
at nightfall. And we say:

the ants have gone home,
but they search on and on and on.

BABA YAGA IN LOVE

Each night, we drew the moon out
to see ourselves: a man and a woman, devouring
blueberries in a clearing.

How magical it is to be full of life! At the market it rained
on us. With my folded hands, he whistled a tune
against sweet, dark grass

and we sang, Wet fingers,
don't you pick my pockets.

THE TRUTH IS

that sadness makes me happy.
Every time a lover dies
in a film, I am happy
in my sadness.

When an old man eats
his breakfast alone,

or a mother can't afford
a sweet bun, a lollipop,

I am sad and happy.

On the news they said
the political prisoner
won't get to see home
for twenty-five years,

an infinity to a fly or an ant

unable to think of anything else
under the wide, blue sky.

It makes me: even sadder
and even happier;

the smell of apples and strawberries
in a milk-warm bath;

a sopping sponge
leaking from the edge of the tub.

FOOD CART

There sulks Selv's food cart, and on it
a package of hotdogs. It empties

and empties until the last is swallowed
at half past eight. The sun drops into the hot-

sauce jar. Selv touches his middle finger
to his lip, then spits. A flame flickers.

Tomorrow, the sun will climb the border
of the jar and stand on its own legs again,

stirring, fevered—reminding
that a new day brings new bread.

GENIE

In a pink hotel room on the blue coast, Arlene tells Peter that she loves music. She keeps "La Vie en Rose" playing on repeat in her apartment. Peter has no records. He likes that Arlene completes him in this sense. In this sense, Arlene also unravels Peter, because he has never spoken about love with anyone, but talking about Edith makes him want to. On the Dreamax bed, between the Sea Salt sheets and Arlene, he feels it. Arlene doesn't feel strongly about it, but at the moment she lifts her palms off the bed to open the bottle of ONEHOPE, she still remembers it. She turns the cork like clockwork. Peter likes to watch the swift movement of Arlene's wrist, but is afraid that if she keeps turning it, her hand may come off like a bottle cap. So Peter turns brave. When Arlene picks up his hand mid-twist and leads him to the centre of the carpet, he clutches the lamp like a microphone and sings. Arlene likes the dance. She likes the fog that rises from the bottle and the salt on Peter's brow. Peter likes his voice against the lamp's hard head. He likes the smell of ONEHOPE, but doesn't care for the fog, which disorients him. Arlene is oriented south. The voice of Edith rises. Peter fixates on the fog and gravity. He doesn't understand why it doesn't fall down the lamp shaft and into his big hands like whipped milk.

A PORTRAIT OF RUSALKA HANGING
FROM A BIRCH TREE

Some trek they took
beneath the tumbling fronds
and up white bark
curled like silvered ribbons.

The weeds wore crinoline
crinkled into a smile.
They walked by where a pail
of cherries spilled onto the wild path
in the outline of a house dress; blown
in with the breeze and stomped on
with black shoes.

R spread it in her crumpled hands
and marked it with round mouth.
How it had changed with her touch
into a forest dress! She showed them:
poppies in a yellow field,
a rowanberry necklace,
a red throat—

and hung the dress on the mountain ash
and herself on the dress.

The weeds proclaimed a death,
the men a coming.

III

Do you know, my lad, do you know?
That from my arms you'll never return?
That with this annihilation
in my arms you'll pay for it?

—Rusalka, Act III, *Rusalka*

SHARPNESS

When I was a pasture, I raised sheep in the chanting fields. There were summoning brooks, green clouds of moss. My father was the earth, my mother the sun, the sheep were my children. My mother fell onto her left side each day, the bells rang high above the hills, light sprouted. Then came more children. When we were hungry, my father turned over, sprigs of wild grasses and dandelions emerged, potatoes and carrots pierced the rock crust. Then: the apocalypse. My children turned pale, but lengthened past us, into the city square. We thought, Let them go, they are growing; let them leave the rain behind. My children took root: their ears straightened like wire, their teeth reached into the ground like wells. Clumps of asphalt grew in my hair. The apocalypse poured through their mouths, and no one heard it arrive. We said, How did we not see their arms extend up our streets and into our houses, which had wind instead of a front, a shadow instead of a back. They threw sticks at my bare feet, clawed at my father, spat nails at my mother. Now, my father can't provide anything. My mother keeps coming back. We don't have a choice to cry wolf, we can only scream him.

YOU FOUND RED AFFECTION

in the hole where I
found an anthill.

I a flower, and you
a bird. I see now—

your raven lashes sprinkled
with russet pollen.

DENTIST

he has every other tooth
removed
by the forest voles
and the weasels

he is restrained, cedar
roots braided with blue spruce
strap him down

it doesn't hurt, he lies

through his remaining teeth
tree sap pours freely

the result of the transfusion
is a viscous howl

forest animals come to him
observe with knotted eyes

stones are dropped
into the pink chinks
to consummate the procedure.

FOREST

I like to think of you as parallel
to what I already know.

In your classroom, the trees
stand upright like pencils,
their leaves are rolled.

They have memorized the wind
and recite its lines,
they drop conjugations
of the bee's ceaseless buzz
and the wolf's howl
like chestnuts. They are versed

in many languages. He who has no birds
for ears, only two sharp tongues for arms,
comes from time to time

to spread black silence. It is
at these great times of need
that the trees stumble,
fall to their knees. Not even Sir
through their once green lips,

not even Amen. It is you
who cuts off their heads, one by one,
with a ray of sun:

a thorough teacher,
harsh and unforgiving.

BRUEGEL'S LENT SPEAKS TO CARNIVAL

You cover up the barren ground
by spitting on it bit by bit: fire-
roasted pork legs, skewered duck, barrels

of sweet mead, pottage that has simmered
over open heat. Most of the villagers
have skipped out of the inns

like calves released to pasture in spring
and they chant in the open square, chain-
dancing to the beats of tambourines

and drums. Some are playing
kubb with branches, chair legs,
brooms; some are begging for coins

and crusted bread. All puff up
their arms and bellies, clear their minds.
And outside the cathedral, the nuns hang

their heads like dried braids of garlic
and cornflowers. What's in a carnival
if not a prelude to desire? The sun drops

chalk dust into our hair
scorched from summer in crimson
and mustard and plum, but the trees

up the street are parched. Nearby,
the fish choke on the oven's
smoke. One hooded man dusts

on his knees—he seems smaller
than a child. In the centre, one
live sow rummages for worms and leaves.

What's in a carnival, if not a prelude
to death? You forgot where it came from,
but they haven't, and when they remind you

about the Creator, you will find
your hands in the dustpan, you will
teach them what it means to
force life to crawl out from its steel mother.

FAITH

It's the thing I can't talk about
when I close my eyes
It collects in my mouth
like snowmelt

ON HOW MY UNCLE RETURNED TO BABEL

When he was older,
my uncle became a weeping baby

but he wasn't always like that.
He used to be many other things:

a plumber, a telephone
repairman,

a whole zoo,
a crowd in which a pigeon

turned in circles and cast spells
on whomever it saw

on its seventh rotation.
Only after did he return
to Babel—

a scientific revelation
the doctors still can't figure out.

But it is simple, look,
a case of linear determinism:

my uncle harboured a fugitive
in his mind,

one too many in his studio
on Paderewski Street.

The thought was born
from a line he read in a very old book.

That same day,
militiamen came knocking
on his door—no,

came knocking down his door:
Look here, we know you're harbouring

somebody here.
No I'm not, he said,

please look around.
They said, Don't play stupid—
tell us exactly where you thought

of keeping them. We know you kept a heavy book
beneath your bed for 67 days

until you returned it to library branch 76438-23…
We even know you took the longer way

to work on April 17 to watch
the cranes return from the east
in triangular formation.

He hadn't yet decided between the cupboard
overlooking the staircase or the rooftop
of the dusty kamienica.

Did you think we wouldn't find out?

When he tried to speak, his words
disintegrated: feathers.

Did you think there'd be no resistance?

The stones he spoke with spilled out
clumsily, bruised his feet.

He spoke with leaves but they stuck
to his tongue like tar.

He spoke with anxious squeaks.

Look now, we know you might believe in Something...

He turned into a grey mouse.

And when they set a trap,
he turned into a lion.

They threw him into the jungle
and called him a killer.

He turned into a phoenix.

They threw him into a fairy tale
and called him a farce.

It must have been 3,000 years later
that, weak and desperate for sleep,
he turned into a child.

They couldn't understand
his babbles.
They petted his soft head.

All was well.

AT LAST YOU'RE HERE

I'll be at the Bird's birthday.
At the table there will be bears,
horses, yellow bats.
I'll put my hair in order, sit
up straight like hard rain.
Come and spread yourselves
out like notes
across the junipers.
A thorn to hold down the evening—
I will grow into the ground.
Pull me out.
Then erase me.
Then erase the bird.

THOUGHTS ON HUMANITY

I sit in the lamp-lit room
reading Solzhenitsyn,
my voice soughing like ash, shuffling like
hemlock in my head,
a wildness that cracks through the windows.

Only the smell of dust and shrapnel
in place of the stars.

TO OUR FUTURE CHILDREN

Last winter we dug out an old fur
coat and carried it to the front porch.
We slept on our stomachs
with our future children.
The wind came through the forest
carrying the beasts' snarling
threats. Their long hair blowing,
the children snored
into the tough white fur. Our hair
stood on end like fire.
The spruce dropped their needles
around us. For one more night,
we kept the beasts howling.

THE WEIGHT

My daughter,
you are small

like a raindrop
in my pocket.

Like a stone
lodged
in my throat.

*

The summer heat killed the mosquitoes—
we have no excuse not to
have supper on the deck tonight.

We leave the books to lean
against the desk,
the laundry dampening on the line,

and meet out on the sun-
burned grass, where chicory and mallow
riffle through loose leaves and roots.

*

Two hours ago, the sun dropped
into the dirt
but it's still bright. I use my hands
as eyeshades.

*

The drought has been peeling
our gardens since April.

The birds are going hungry,
the trees have lost their hair.
But the papers report that
the apples are sweeter.

*

I listen in:

what's in a fruit if not the end
of the start of the end
ask its seeds

the tree is silent

*

A neighbour rolls his bike over
our collapsed mesh fence

he asks if we have a plan B
(we don't).

*

For our supper?
For our earth?

*

If we had to live
on the food from our garden
on the milk from our cows

(we should)

Plan B would be walking
the cows to the stream.

Plan B would be turning into grass.

*

We sit in silence. We turn into ears
of corn.

       *

The unpredicted rain
falls from the vacant sky.

The birds take air
into their bodies.

       *

Between small bites of watercress, rose
petals, melon pear

I learn what it's like to hold something
larger than myself.

LESSONS IN PHILOSOPHY

My daughter draws yellow suns
across the page of a rust-red notebook.
Some are concentric, some layered.
Some have rays. Some have edges
like cracked bones. Some are skewered meat.

The longest stretches diagonally
past the corners of the notebook
and onto the stainless steel. I don't know
where to look on a page like this.
I generally see only one sun at a time.

But once I caught two—one in each
eye—on a sweltering summer evening.
Even then, it was the same one, separated
long enough to catch its reflection
before descending into the riverbank's

bowing grass. I imagine Plato sitting down
to cry at the sight of this.
He yanks off his arm in rage,
screams Blood—
how could anyone fuck him over like this
when his theories of knowledge
only ever spoke about one reality,
one yellow sun in the clear sky!

I try to decide where to focus my eyes
between the 37 dissected suns, the big tree,
the bigger dog, the clouds
outside our window that are clearly
hungry, crackling at us
like fireworks.

My daughter yells "Another!"
I don't know if this time
it's for a new piece of paper
or still another sun.

RUSALKA KISSES THE PRINCE

1. When you found me again, we tried to make soup, but itturned into pond water.
2. Frogs emerged, shivering.
3. We ate green currants against the fence.
4. We twisted our faces toward the pale face of the sun.
5. We stood over burning wood.
6. The bread emerged pink, screaming.
7. Our hair darkened, fireflies didn't alight on it.
8. We hopped barefoot over meadows, but the dew didn't wash our feet. The moon didn't shoe them in gold slippers.
9. Over steaming waters, we became tangled in water lilies.
10. The night said: For you, I will cry. But not like an ocean. I will cry like wildfire
11. We trembled behind God. We answered with a kiss.
12. We stood because we kept standing in darkness.
13. Now in front of him, we tremble still.

CADMIUM RED

This must be what being
the lover means

Fell in a poem
got lost in the woods
along the way

somebody gave a kiss

and it was
the most
cardinal kiss

under naked branches

Your palms:

snow
on white petals

bloodstains
on my knees.

RUSALKA STAINED

When they ask how we met, I'll say I washed your poem that was dark and crumpled, that had fallen into the ravine behind our stick houses. That's how it was, wasn't it? I picked it up off your desk without thinking, shoved it into a jean pocket. I didn't mean to take anything from it, only to straighten it out into something recognizable. Sometimes we convince ourselves that things need saving. The next day, when I woke up, mine was washed too. It stained your hands, a dark red like wolfberries. We laughed about it like maniacs. You rubbed your hands on things to get rid of the pigment: my face, the cushions, your boxers, my Alice-blue breasts. Instead, it just spread to everything you touched. I thought that was it for the poem, a poem for the dogs now. But somehow, it survived: shinier, more translucent. Each word firmly anchored in its place. Since then we've washed lots of things, for bad or for good. We boiled bones in big pots and made crying soup. We picked snails off the sidewalk. We prayed in temples that felt good because they didn't feel right. We joined dirty hands, wrote new poems. They were darker still.

TWO ENDS OF A ROOF

A woman and a man
hold up two ends of a roof,
but the rain is flowing
from the ground up: the drowning
kettle screams, the wind tears at the arms
of the hanging parkas. Even the painting
has been pulled into the mud,
unrecognizable.

This is the life they know: If there's time
for kindness, there's time
for suffering—a landslide
revelation. It floods the walls.
Or an old tube of toothpaste,
clotted at the top but
half-empty.

And this is what they do:
one hand holds the roof,
one holds the other's
splitting back.

"All that sunshine will make us crazy," said the old florist
looking out the window,
and squeezed my untrained hands
until they ripened. And suddenly
I had to cry.
I could just barely hear

the music dying.

CLEARING

The spruces are ill and their needles
are falling. They are bleached like straw,
spilling at the feet
of the trees. In a hotel room
in downtown Marrakech
I remember us sitting on a white bed by a window
overlooking a pool. You said, If only
we could be in the desert—
I'd show you roses as strong
as disease, brown as rust.

Back then, I hadn't yet caught
your love of grieving. Now
years later I'm out under a nettle-
laced sky tearing through the mulch
beside you. Whole days and nights. My hands
doing only rough work, and that's the softest thing
I can think of.

OATH OF MODERN-DAY RUSALKA

I'm 27 and still becoming
what I will become. All I really want
is to not become loving
or kind.

But if I love, I'll love
exactly, in its plain definition.

I won't become a good wife or a great
lover. I will make love the obvious way
like trembling grass,
like a dog's tail.

As to kindness:
I'll be the kind of woman
who pulls at the lean shadow of a spruce
long after it has fallen into the night.

Other things I will or won't be:

A thrashing bird. If I'm a bird, I'll be a bird:
that flies, thrashes, chirps.

A littered windowsill: I may be a windowsill
that holds plants, a candle, books
that are used daily, that flutter in stillness.

I won't become a chimney,
bright red or covered
in soot. Just a chimney that is a cat
wrapped around itself

like fog.
I can be a monster too.
If I scare anyone, let me
be a tree that scares anyone instead.

I don't have to be physical.
I don't have to have colour or structure
in the soft of a palm; I can be air
that lives inside one lung
then pushes into another.
I will be the pushing.

I will be a verb, a zoo, shoe leather
after rain. At the very least,
I won't become an adjective.

ACKNOWLEDGEMENTS

Many thanks to the editors of the following publications, in which a selection of these poems first appeared (some in revised form): *The Rusty Toque, Puritan Magazine, December Magazine, Nine Mile Magazine, Artis Magazine, The Café Review.*

I owe much gratitude to Tyler Erlendson and Michael Mirolla, who have helped shape this manuscript at various stages.

Thanks to Sandra Alcosser, Eduardo C. Corral, and Marvin Bell for their advice and mentorship as this book was beginning to take form.

Much thanks to my on-the-page teachers, whose work has guided and influenced the language of these poems: Julian Kornhauser, Valzhyna Mort, Venus Khoury-Ghata, Adam Zagajewski, Ilya Kaminsky, Yehuda Amichai, and countless others.

Thank you to the professors and staff at Pacific University, where many of these poems were made.

Many thanks to the extraordinary Stuart Ross for his dedication and scrupulous edits, and to Brian Kaufman and Karen Green of Anvil Press for their support of this book. Thank you to Clint Hutzulak for the cover design.

Thank you to my parents for their love and support.

Finally: thanks to my husband, Taylor, who is present in every poem; who keeps reminding me that the simple things are sometimes the most difficult, always the most compelling.

NOTES

Many of the poems in this book would not exist without the influence of (and dialogue with) other poets, both past and contemporary:

"Melodies": "lowering tray of mist" is adapted from Valzyna Mort's poem "Stach Rex": "Your horse carries its head on the tray of mist/and runs until its teeth start aching."

"Binoculars" was written as an imitation of Ruth Stone's "Lighter Than Air."

"The Imaginary Town of Grimm": select lines from sections IV and VII adapted from Venus Khoury-Ghata's "Interments" (from *Nettles*).

"Citadel" was written as a response to Vasko Popa's "Village of My Ancestors."

"A Portrait of Serving Girls as Nightingales": the image "a rooster spits devotions into the sky's sleeping throat/then loses his head" is drawn from Valzhyna Mort's "Mocking Bird Hotel": "a rooster repeats hallelujah! until it loses its head."

"Letter to a Real Town: III": inspired by Bertolt Brecht's "Of Poor B.B."

"The Thorn and the Washbasin": images in the third stanza compiled from various sections of Venus Khoury Ghata's "Interments" (from *Nettles*).

"Animal Park": the line "who didn't notice they were dead" is drawn from Adam Zagajewski's "Luxembourg Gardens": "they don't recall all those who once/strolled their avenues, who haven't noticed that they're dead," and "plumes of sun" is an image drawn from "Impassive" (both from *Unseen Hand*).

"Baba Yaga in Love" was written as an imitation of the following section from Ilya Kaminsky's "Natalia":

And each night, looking up, we saw ourselves:
a man and a woman, whispering Lord,
one word the soul destroys to make clear.

How magical it is to live! it rained at the market,
with my fingers, she tapped out her iambics
on the back of our largest casserole

and we sang, Sweet dollars,
why aren't you in my pockets?

"Sharpness": "let them leave the rain behind" quoted from Venus Khoury-Ghata's "Interments" (from *Nettles*).

"Forest": "I like to think of you as parallel to what I already know" adapted from Tracy K. Smith's "My God, It's Full of Stars": "We like to think of it as parallel to what we know."

"At Last You're Here": written as an imitation of Ilhan Berk's "We Knew the World As Long-Held Kisses and Embraces" from *Madrigals*.

"Knowledge": written as an imitation of Jean Follain's "Life."

"To Our Future Children": inspired by Ruth Stone's "Green Apples."

"Two Ends of a Roof": "If there's time for kindness, there's time for suffering" is adapted from Guillaume Apollinaire's "The Hills": "there will be time for suffering/there will be time for kindness," "beauty will be made of suffering and kindness."

Anna van Valkenburg was born in Konin, Poland, and currently lives in Mississauga. Her poetry and reviews have been featured in many periodicals, including *The Puritan*, *Prism International*, *December Magazine*, and *The Rusty Toque*. Her work has been shortlisted for the Pangolin Poetry Prize and nominated for the AWP Intro Journals Project. Anna is the associate publisher at Guernica Editions. *Queen and Carcass* is her first poetry collection.

OTHER FEED DOG BOOKS FROM ANVIL PRESS

"A Feed Dog Book" is an imprint of Anvil Press edited by Stuart Ross and dedicated to contemporary poetry under the influence of surrealism. We are particularly interested in seeing such manuscripts from members of diverse and marginalized communities. Write Stuart at razovsky@gmail.com.

The Least You Can Do Is Be Magnificent: New & Selected Writings of Steve Venright, compiled and with an afterword by Alessandro Porco (2017)
I Heard Something, by Jaime Forsythe (2018)
On the Count of None, by Allison Chisholm (2018)
The Inflatable Life, by Mark Laba (2019)
Float and Scurry, by Heather Birrell (2019)
The Headless Man, by Peter Dubé (2020)

an imprint of Anvil Press